50 Sweet Treats & Classic Bakes Recipes

By: Kelly Johnson

Table of Contents

- Chocolate Chip Cookies
- Sugar Cookies
- Snickerdoodles
- Oatmeal Raisin Cookies
- Peanut Butter Cookies
- Shortbread Cookies
- Double Chocolate Cookies
- Gingerbread Cookies
- Almond Biscotti
- Linzer Cookies
- Brownies
- Blondies
- Chocolate Lava Cake
- New York-Style Cheesecake
- Japanese Cotton Cheesecake
- Classic Carrot Cake
- Red Velvet Cake
- Black Forest Cake
- Tiramisu
- Tres Leches Cake
- Pound Cake
- Angel Food Cake
- Lemon Drizzle Cake
- Victoria Sponge Cake
- Funfetti Cake
- German Chocolate Cake
- Coconut Cake
- Strawberry Shortcake
- Banana Bread
- Apple Crumble
- Classic Apple Pie
- Pecan Pie
- Pumpkin Pie
- Lemon Tart
- Chocolate Tart

- Éclairs
- Profiteroles
- Cream Puffs
- Macarons
- Cannoli
- Baklava
- Sticky Toffee Pudding
- Molten Chocolate Cake
- Cinnamon Rolls
- Brioche Buns
- Danish Pastries
- Croissants
- Scones
- Churros with Chocolate Sauce
- Madeleine Cakes

Chocolate Chip Cookies

Ingredients:

- 1 cup unsalted butter, softened
- 1 cup brown sugar
- ½ cup granulated sugar
- 2 eggs
- 2 tsp vanilla extract
- 2 ¼ cups all-purpose flour
- 1 tsp baking soda
- ½ tsp salt
- 2 cups chocolate chips

Instructions:

1. Preheat oven to 350°F (175°C).
2. Cream butter, brown sugar, and granulated sugar.
3. Add eggs and vanilla, mixing until combined.
4. Stir in flour, baking soda, and salt.
5. Fold in chocolate chips.
6. Drop spoonfuls onto a baking sheet and bake for 10–12 minutes.

Sugar Cookies

Ingredients:

- 1 cup unsalted butter, softened
- 1 cup granulated sugar
- 1 egg
- 1 tsp vanilla extract
- 2 ¾ cups all-purpose flour
- 1 tsp baking powder
- ½ tsp salt

Instructions:

1. Preheat oven to 350°F (175°C).
2. Cream butter and sugar. Add egg and vanilla.
3. Stir in flour, baking powder, and salt.
4. Roll out dough and cut into shapes.
5. Bake for 8–10 minutes.

Snickerdoodles

Ingredients:

- 1 cup unsalted butter, softened
- 1 ½ cups sugar
- 2 eggs
- 2 ¾ cups all-purpose flour
- 2 tsp cream of tartar
- 1 tsp baking soda
- ½ tsp salt
- 2 tbsp sugar + 1 tsp cinnamon (for rolling)

Instructions:

1. Preheat oven to 375°F (190°C).
2. Cream butter and sugar. Add eggs.
3. Stir in flour, cream of tartar, baking soda, and salt.
4. Roll dough into balls, coat in cinnamon-sugar mixture.
5. Bake for 10–12 minutes.

Oatmeal Raisin Cookies

Ingredients:

- 1 cup unsalted butter, softened
- 1 cup brown sugar
- ½ cup granulated sugar
- 2 eggs
- 2 tsp vanilla extract
- 1 ½ cups all-purpose flour
- 1 tsp baking soda
- 1 tsp cinnamon
- ½ tsp salt
- 3 cups oats
- 1 cup raisins

Instructions:

1. Preheat oven to 350°F (175°C).
2. Cream butter, brown sugar, and granulated sugar.
3. Add eggs and vanilla.
4. Stir in flour, baking soda, cinnamon, and salt.
5. Fold in oats and raisins.
6. Drop spoonfuls onto a baking sheet and bake for 10–12 minutes.

Peanut Butter Cookies

Ingredients:

- 1 cup peanut butter
- ½ cup unsalted butter, softened
- 1 cup granulated sugar
- ½ cup brown sugar
- 1 egg
- 1 ½ cups all-purpose flour
- 1 tsp baking soda
- ½ tsp salt

Instructions:

1. Preheat oven to 350°F (175°C).
2. Cream peanut butter, butter, and sugars.
3. Add egg and mix well.
4. Stir in flour, baking soda, and salt.
5. Roll into balls, press with a fork, and bake for 10–12 minutes.

Shortbread Cookies

Ingredients:

- 1 cup unsalted butter, softened
- ½ cup powdered sugar
- 2 cups all-purpose flour
- ¼ tsp salt

Instructions:

1. Preheat oven to 325°F (163°C).
2. Cream butter and powdered sugar.
3. Stir in flour and salt.
4. Roll dough, cut into shapes, and bake for 12–15 minutes.

Double Chocolate Cookies

Ingredients:

- 1 cup unsalted butter, softened
- 1 cup brown sugar
- ½ cup granulated sugar
- 2 eggs
- 1 tsp vanilla extract
- 2 cups all-purpose flour
- ½ cup cocoa powder
- 1 tsp baking soda
- ½ tsp salt
- 1 ½ cups chocolate chips

Instructions:

1. Preheat oven to 350°F (175°C).
2. Cream butter, brown sugar, and granulated sugar.
3. Add eggs and vanilla.
4. Stir in flour, cocoa powder, baking soda, and salt.
5. Fold in chocolate chips.
6. Drop spoonfuls onto a baking sheet and bake for 10–12 minutes.

Gingerbread Cookies

Ingredients:

- ¾ cup unsalted butter, softened
- ¾ cup brown sugar
- 1 egg
- ½ cup molasses
- 3 cups all-purpose flour
- 1 tbsp ground ginger
- 1 tsp cinnamon
- ½ tsp cloves
- ½ tsp baking soda
- ½ tsp salt

Instructions:

1. Preheat oven to 350°F (175°C).
2. Cream butter and brown sugar. Add egg and molasses.
3. Stir in flour, spices, baking soda, and salt.
4. Roll out dough, cut into shapes, and bake for 8–10 minutes.

Almond Biscotti

Ingredients:

- 2 cups all-purpose flour
- 1 cup sugar
- 1 tsp baking powder
- ¼ tsp salt
- 3 eggs
- 1 tsp almond extract
- 1 cup almonds (chopped)

Instructions:

1. Preheat oven to 350°F (175°C).
2. Mix flour, sugar, baking powder, and salt.
3. Add eggs and almond extract, mixing to form dough.
4. Stir in almonds.
5. Shape into logs and bake for 25 minutes.
6. Slice into biscotti and bake for 10 more minutes.

Linzer Cookies

Ingredients:

- 1 cup unsalted butter, softened
- ½ cup powdered sugar
- 1 egg yolk
- 1 tsp vanilla extract
- 2 cups all-purpose flour
- ½ tsp cinnamon
- ½ cup ground almonds
- ½ cup raspberry jam
- Powdered sugar for dusting

Instructions:

1. Preheat oven to 350°F (175°C).
2. Cream butter and powdered sugar. Add egg yolk and vanilla.
3. Stir in flour, cinnamon, and ground almonds.
4. Roll out dough, cut out shapes, and cut centers from half.
5. Bake for 10–12 minutes.
6. Spread jam on whole cookies and top with cut-out ones.
7. Dust with powdered sugar.

Brownies

Ingredients:

- 1 cup unsalted butter, melted
- 2 cups granulated sugar
- 4 eggs
- 2 tsp vanilla extract
- 1 cup all-purpose flour
- ½ cup cocoa powder
- ½ tsp salt
- ½ tsp baking powder

Instructions:

1. Preheat oven to 350°F (175°C). Grease a baking pan.
2. Mix melted butter and sugar. Add eggs and vanilla.
3. Stir in flour, cocoa powder, salt, and baking powder.
4. Pour into pan and bake for 25–30 minutes.
5. Let cool before cutting.

Blondies

Ingredients:

- 1 cup unsalted butter, melted
- 1 ½ cups brown sugar
- 2 eggs
- 2 tsp vanilla extract
- 2 cups all-purpose flour
- 1 tsp baking powder
- ½ tsp salt
- 1 cup chocolate chips or nuts (optional)

Instructions:

1. Preheat oven to 350°F (175°C). Grease a baking pan.
2. Mix melted butter and brown sugar. Add eggs and vanilla.
3. Stir in flour, baking powder, and salt.
4. Fold in chocolate chips or nuts if using.
5. Bake for 25–30 minutes. Let cool before cutting.

Chocolate Lava Cake

Ingredients:

- ½ cup unsalted butter
- 4 oz dark chocolate, chopped
- 2 eggs
- 2 egg yolks
- ¼ cup sugar
- 2 tbsp all-purpose flour

Instructions:

1. Preheat oven to 425°F (220°C). Grease ramekins.
2. Melt butter and chocolate together.
3. Whisk eggs, egg yolks, and sugar until light.
4. Stir in melted chocolate and flour.
5. Divide into ramekins and bake for 10–12 minutes.
6. Serve warm with ice cream.

New York-Style Cheesecake

Ingredients:

- 2 cups graham cracker crumbs
- ½ cup melted butter
- 24 oz cream cheese, softened
- 1 cup sugar
- 3 eggs
- 1 tsp vanilla extract
- 1 cup sour cream

Instructions:

1. Preheat oven to 325°F (163°C). Mix graham cracker crumbs and butter, press into a pan.
2. Beat cream cheese and sugar until smooth.
3. Add eggs one at a time, then vanilla and sour cream.
4. Pour over crust and bake for 50–60 minutes.
5. Let cool and chill before serving.

Japanese Cotton Cheesecake

Ingredients:

- 8 oz cream cheese, softened
- 2 tbsp butter
- ½ cup milk
- 6 eggs, separated
- ½ cup sugar
- ½ cup cake flour
- 2 tbsp cornstarch

Instructions:

1. Preheat oven to 320°F (160°C). Line a cake pan.
2. Melt cream cheese, butter, and milk together.
3. Stir in egg yolks, flour, and cornstarch.
4. Beat egg whites and sugar into stiff peaks, fold into batter.
5. Bake in a water bath for 60 minutes.

Classic Carrot Cake

Ingredients:

- 2 cups all-purpose flour
- 2 cups sugar
- 1 tsp baking soda
- 1 ½ tsp cinnamon
- ½ tsp salt
- 1 cup vegetable oil
- 4 eggs
- 3 cups grated carrots
- ½ cup chopped nuts (optional)

Instructions:

1. Preheat oven to 350°F (175°C). Grease cake pans.
2. Mix flour, sugar, baking soda, cinnamon, and salt.
3. Add oil and eggs, mix well. Stir in carrots and nuts.
4. Pour into pans and bake for 30–35 minutes.

Red Velvet Cake

Ingredients:

- 2 ½ cups all-purpose flour
- 1 ½ cups sugar
- 1 tsp baking soda
- 1 tsp cocoa powder
- 1 cup buttermilk
- 1 cup vegetable oil
- 2 eggs
- 2 tsp vanilla extract
- 1 tbsp red food coloring

Instructions:

1. Preheat oven to 350°F (175°C). Grease cake pans.
2. Mix flour, sugar, baking soda, and cocoa.
3. Add buttermilk, oil, eggs, vanilla, and food coloring.
4. Pour into pans and bake for 30 minutes.

Black Forest Cake

Ingredients:

- 2 cups all-purpose flour
- 2 cups sugar
- ¾ cup cocoa powder
- 2 tsp baking soda
- 1 tsp baking powder
- 1 cup buttermilk
- ½ cup vegetable oil
- 2 eggs
- 1 tsp vanilla extract
- 1 cup hot water
- 1 cup cherry filling

Instructions:

1. Preheat oven to 350°F (175°C). Grease cake pans.
2. Mix flour, sugar, cocoa, baking soda, and baking powder.
3. Add buttermilk, oil, eggs, and vanilla. Stir in hot water.
4. Pour into pans and bake for 30 minutes.
5. Layer with cherry filling and whipped cream.

Tiramisu

Ingredients:

- 1 cup brewed espresso
- 3 egg yolks
- ½ cup sugar
- 8 oz mascarpone cheese
- ¾ cup heavy cream
- 24 ladyfingers
- Cocoa powder for dusting

Instructions:

1. Beat egg yolks and sugar until thick.
2. Fold in mascarpone cheese.
3. Whip heavy cream and fold into mascarpone mixture.
4. Dip ladyfingers in espresso, layer with mascarpone cream.
5. Repeat layers and dust with cocoa powder.
6. Chill before serving.

Tres Leches Cake

Ingredients:

- 1 cup all-purpose flour
- 1 cup sugar
- 1 tsp baking powder
- 5 eggs
- ⅓ cup milk
- 1 can evaporated milk
- 1 can sweetened condensed milk
- ½ cup heavy cream

Instructions:

1. Preheat oven to 350°F (175°C). Grease cake pan.
2. Beat eggs and sugar until fluffy.
3. Stir in flour, baking powder, and milk.
4. Pour into pan and bake for 30 minutes.
5. Mix evaporated milk, condensed milk, and heavy cream.
6. Pour over warm cake and chill before serving.

Pound Cake

Ingredients:

- 1 cup unsalted butter, softened
- 2 cups granulated sugar
- 4 eggs
- 2 tsp vanilla extract
- 3 cups all-purpose flour
- ½ tsp baking powder
- ½ tsp salt
- 1 cup whole milk

Instructions:

1. Preheat oven to 350°F (175°C). Grease a loaf pan.
2. Cream butter and sugar until light and fluffy.
3. Add eggs one at a time, then vanilla.
4. Mix in flour, baking powder, and salt, alternating with milk.
5. Pour into pan and bake for 60–70 minutes.

Angel Food Cake

Ingredients:

- 1 cup cake flour
- 1 ½ cups granulated sugar
- 12 egg whites
- 1 ½ tsp cream of tartar
- 1 tsp vanilla extract
- ¼ tsp salt

Instructions:

1. Preheat oven to 350°F (175°C). Do not grease the pan.
2. Beat egg whites, cream of tartar, and salt until soft peaks form.
3. Gradually add sugar and beat until stiff peaks form.
4. Gently fold in vanilla and sifted flour.
5. Pour into an ungreased tube pan and bake for 35–40 minutes.

Lemon Drizzle Cake

Ingredients:

- 1 cup unsalted butter, softened
- 1 cup granulated sugar
- 2 eggs
- 1 ½ cups all-purpose flour
- 1 ½ tsp baking powder
- Zest of 1 lemon
- ½ cup milk

For the drizzle:

- Juice of 1 lemon
- ½ cup powdered sugar

Instructions:

1. Preheat oven to 350°F (175°C). Grease a loaf pan.
2. Beat butter and sugar until fluffy. Add eggs one at a time.
3. Mix in flour, baking powder, and lemon zest, alternating with milk.
4. Pour into pan and bake for 40–45 minutes.
5. Mix lemon juice and powdered sugar for drizzle and pour over warm cake.

Victoria Sponge Cake

Ingredients:

- 1 cup unsalted butter, softened
- 1 cup granulated sugar
- 4 eggs
- 2 cups self-rising flour
- 1 tsp vanilla extract
- ¼ cup milk
- ½ cup strawberry jam
- ½ cup whipped cream
- Powdered sugar for dusting

Instructions:

1. Preheat oven to 350°F (175°C). Grease two round cake pans.
2. Cream butter and sugar, then add eggs one at a time.
3. Fold in flour, vanilla, and milk.
4. Divide batter between pans and bake for 25–30 minutes.
5. Cool and sandwich with jam and whipped cream. Dust with powdered sugar.

Funfetti Cake

Ingredients:

- 2 ½ cups all-purpose flour
- 1 ½ cups sugar
- 1 tbsp baking powder
- ½ tsp salt
- 1 cup whole milk
- ½ cup unsalted butter, softened
- 3 eggs
- 1 tbsp vanilla extract
- ½ cup rainbow sprinkles

Instructions:

1. Preheat oven to 350°F (175°C). Grease cake pans.
2. Mix flour, sugar, baking powder, and salt.
3. Add milk, butter, eggs, and vanilla. Beat until smooth.
4. Fold in sprinkles.
5. Bake for 25–30 minutes.

German Chocolate Cake

Ingredients:

- 2 cups all-purpose flour
- 1 ½ cups sugar
- ¾ cup cocoa powder
- 1 tsp baking soda
- 1 tsp baking powder
- ½ tsp salt
- 1 cup buttermilk
- ½ cup vegetable oil
- 2 eggs
- 1 tsp vanilla extract

For the frosting:

- 1 cup evaporated milk
- 1 cup sugar
- 3 egg yolks
- ½ cup butter
- 1 cup shredded coconut
- 1 cup chopped pecans

Instructions:

1. Preheat oven to 350°F (175°C). Grease cake pans.
2. Mix flour, sugar, cocoa, baking soda, baking powder, and salt.
3. Add buttermilk, oil, eggs, and vanilla. Mix well.
4. Pour into pans and bake for 30 minutes.
5. For frosting, cook evaporated milk, sugar, egg yolks, and butter until thick. Stir in coconut and pecans.

Coconut Cake

Ingredients:

- 2 ½ cups all-purpose flour
- 1 tsp baking powder
- ½ tsp baking soda
- 1 cup unsalted butter, softened
- 2 cups sugar
- 4 eggs
- 1 cup coconut milk
- 1 cup shredded coconut

Instructions:

1. Preheat oven to 350°F (175°C). Grease cake pans.
2. Cream butter and sugar, then add eggs one at a time.
3. Mix in dry ingredients, alternating with coconut milk.
4. Fold in shredded coconut.
5. Bake for 30–35 minutes.

Strawberry Shortcake

Ingredients:

- 2 cups all-purpose flour
- ¼ cup sugar
- 1 tbsp baking powder
- ½ tsp salt
- ½ cup cold butter, cubed
- ¾ cup heavy cream
- 1 tsp vanilla extract
- 2 cups strawberries, sliced
- ½ cup whipped cream

Instructions:

1. Preheat oven to 400°F (200°C). Grease a baking sheet.
2. Mix flour, sugar, baking powder, and salt. Cut in butter.
3. Add cream and vanilla, mix until dough forms.
4. Shape into rounds and bake for 15–18 minutes.
5. Split biscuits and layer with strawberries and whipped cream.

Banana Bread

Ingredients:

- 2 cups all-purpose flour
- 1 tsp baking soda
- ½ tsp salt
- ½ cup unsalted butter, melted
- ¾ cup brown sugar
- 2 eggs
- 3 ripe bananas, mashed
- 1 tsp vanilla extract

Instructions:

1. Preheat oven to 350°F (175°C). Grease a loaf pan.
2. Mix flour, baking soda, and salt.
3. Stir in melted butter, brown sugar, eggs, bananas, and vanilla.
4. Pour into pan and bake for 50–60 minutes.

Apple Crumble

Ingredients:

- 4 apples, peeled and sliced
- ½ cup sugar
- 1 tsp cinnamon
- 1 cup all-purpose flour
- ½ cup brown sugar
- ½ cup butter, melted

Instructions:

1. Preheat oven to 375°F (190°C). Grease a baking dish.
2. Toss apples with sugar and cinnamon, place in dish.
3. Mix flour, brown sugar, and melted butter for crumble topping.
4. Sprinkle over apples and bake for 30–35 minutes.

Classic Apple Pie

Ingredients:

- 2 pie crusts
- 6 apples, peeled and sliced
- ¾ cup sugar
- 1 tsp cinnamon
- 2 tbsp flour
- 1 tbsp lemon juice

Instructions:

1. Preheat oven to 375°F (190°C).
2. Toss apples with sugar, cinnamon, flour, and lemon juice.
3. Place one crust in a pie dish, fill with apple mixture.
4. Top with second crust, seal edges, and cut vents.
5. Bake for 45–50 minutes.

Pecan Pie

Ingredients:

- 1 unbaked pie crust
- 1 cup corn syrup
- 1 cup brown sugar
- 3 eggs
- ½ cup unsalted butter, melted
- 1 tsp vanilla extract
- 1 ½ cups pecans

Instructions:

1. Preheat oven to 350°F (175°C).
2. Whisk corn syrup, brown sugar, eggs, melted butter, and vanilla.
3. Stir in pecans and pour into the pie crust.
4. Bake for 50–55 minutes.

Pumpkin Pie

Ingredients:

- 1 unbaked pie crust
- 1 can (15 oz) pumpkin puree
- ¾ cup brown sugar
- 2 eggs
- 1 cup heavy cream
- 1 tsp cinnamon
- ½ tsp nutmeg
- ½ tsp ginger

Instructions:

1. Preheat oven to 375°F (190°C).
2. Whisk pumpkin, sugar, eggs, cream, and spices.
3. Pour into pie crust and bake for 50–55 minutes.

Lemon Tart

Ingredients:

- 1 tart crust
- ¾ cup lemon juice
- 1 cup sugar
- 4 eggs
- ½ cup heavy cream
- Zest of 1 lemon

Instructions:

1. Preheat oven to 350°F (175°C).
2. Whisk lemon juice, sugar, eggs, cream, and zest.
3. Pour into crust and bake for 25–30 minutes.

Chocolate Tart

Ingredients:

- 1 tart crust
- 8 oz dark chocolate
- 1 cup heavy cream
- 2 tbsp sugar
- 1 tsp vanilla extract

Instructions:

1. Heat cream and sugar until simmering.
2. Pour over chopped chocolate and stir until smooth.
3. Add vanilla, pour into crust, and chill for 2 hours.

Éclairs

Ingredients:

- ½ cup butter
- 1 cup water
- 1 cup flour
- 4 eggs

For filling:

- 2 cups pastry cream

For glaze:

- 4 oz chocolate
- ½ cup heavy cream

Instructions:

1. Preheat oven to 375°F (190°C).
2. Heat butter and water, stir in flour, then beat in eggs.
3. Pipe onto baking sheet and bake for 25 minutes.
4. Fill with pastry cream and glaze with melted chocolate.

Profiteroles

Same as éclairs, but filled with ice cream instead of pastry cream.

Cream Puffs

Same as éclairs, but filled with whipped cream instead of pastry cream.

Macarons

Ingredients:

- 1 cup almond flour
- 1 ½ cups powdered sugar
- 3 egg whites
- ¼ cup granulated sugar

Instructions:

1. Whisk egg whites with sugar until stiff peaks form.
2. Fold in almond flour and powdered sugar.
3. Pipe onto parchment paper and rest for 30 minutes.
4. Bake at 300°F (150°C) for 12–15 minutes.
5. Fill with buttercream or ganache.

Cannoli

Ingredients:

- 2 cups flour
- ¼ cup sugar
- 1 tsp cinnamon
- ¼ cup butter
- 1 egg
- ½ cup white wine

For filling:

- 1 cup ricotta
- ½ cup powdered sugar
- 1 tsp vanilla

Instructions:

1. Mix dough, roll thin, and cut into circles.
2. Wrap around cannoli tubes and fry at 350°F (175°C) until golden.
3. Mix ricotta, sugar, and vanilla, and pipe into shells.

Baklava

Ingredients:

- 1 package phyllo dough
- 2 cups chopped nuts
- ½ cup sugar
- 1 tsp cinnamon
- 1 cup butter, melted
- 1 cup honey

Instructions:

1. Layer phyllo sheets, brushing each with butter.
2. Sprinkle nut mixture every few layers.
3. Bake at 350°F (175°C) for 40 minutes.
4. Drizzle with honey.

Sticky Toffee Pudding

Ingredients:

- 1 cup dates, chopped
- 1 cup boiling water
- 1 tsp baking soda
- ½ cup butter
- ¾ cup brown sugar
- 2 eggs
- 1 ½ cups flour

For sauce:

- ½ cup butter
- 1 cup brown sugar
- ½ cup heavy cream

Instructions:

1. Soak dates in boiling water with baking soda.
2. Beat butter and sugar, add eggs, then mix in flour and date mixture.
3. Bake at 350°F (175°C) for 30 minutes.
4. Simmer sauce ingredients and pour over warm cake.

Molten Chocolate Cake

Ingredients:

- ½ cup butter
- 4 oz dark chocolate
- 2 eggs
- 2 egg yolks
- ¼ cup sugar
- 2 tbsp flour

Instructions:

1. Melt butter and chocolate.
2. Whisk eggs, yolks, and sugar, then mix in chocolate.
3. Fold in flour and bake at 425°F (220°C) for 10–12 minutes.

Cinnamon Rolls

Ingredients:

For the dough:

- 2 ¾ cups flour
- ¼ cup sugar
- 1 packet (2 ¼ tsp) yeast
- ½ cup warm milk
- ¼ cup unsalted butter, melted
- 1 egg
- ½ tsp salt

For the filling:

- ⅓ cup butter, softened
- ½ cup brown sugar
- 1 tbsp cinnamon

For the glaze:

- 1 cup powdered sugar
- 2 tbsp milk
- ½ tsp vanilla

Instructions:

1. Combine flour, sugar, and yeast. Add warm milk, melted butter, egg, and salt. Knead until smooth.
2. Let rise for 1 hour. Roll into a rectangle and spread with butter.
3. Mix brown sugar and cinnamon, then sprinkle over dough. Roll tightly and cut into slices.
4. Place in a greased pan, cover, and let rise for 30 minutes.
5. Bake at 350°F (175°C) for 20–25 minutes.
6. Drizzle with glaze.

Brioche Buns

Ingredients:

- 3 ½ cups flour
- ¼ cup sugar
- 1 packet (2 ¼ tsp) yeast
- ¾ cup warm milk
- 3 eggs
- 1 tsp salt
- ½ cup butter, softened

Instructions:

1. Mix flour, sugar, and yeast. Add warm milk, eggs, and salt. Knead until smooth.
2. Gradually add butter while kneading. Let rise for 2 hours.
3. Shape into buns and place on a baking sheet. Let rise for 1 hour.
4. Brush with egg wash and bake at 375°F (190°C) for 15–20 minutes.

Danish Pastries

Ingredients:

- 2 cups flour
- 2 tbsp sugar
- ½ tsp salt
- 1 packet (2 ¼ tsp) yeast
- ½ cup warm milk
- 1 egg
- ½ cup butter, cold
- ½ cup fruit preserves or pastry cream

Instructions:

1. Mix flour, sugar, salt, and yeast. Add warm milk and egg, knead lightly.
2. Roll dough out and layer with butter, folding and chilling between folds.
3. Roll and cut into shapes, fill with fruit preserves or pastry cream.
4. Let rise for 30 minutes, then bake at 375°F (190°C) for 15–20 minutes.

Croissants

Ingredients:

- 2 ¼ tsp yeast
- 3 tbsp warm water
- 3 ½ cups flour
- 1 cup milk
- ¼ cup sugar
- 1 tsp salt
- 1 cup butter, cold
- 1 egg (for egg wash)

Instructions:

1. Dissolve yeast in warm water. Mix with flour, milk, sugar, and salt. Knead lightly.
2. Roll dough into a rectangle, place butter in the center, fold over, and chill.
3. Roll and fold 3 times, chilling between folds.
4. Roll out, cut into triangles, and roll into croissant shapes.
5. Let rise for 2 hours, brush with egg wash, and bake at 375°F (190°C) for 18–20 minutes.

Scones

Ingredients:

- 2 cups flour
- ¼ cup sugar
- 1 tbsp baking powder
- ½ tsp salt
- ½ cup butter, cold and cubed
- ½ cup heavy cream
- 1 egg
- ½ tsp vanilla

Instructions:

1. Preheat oven to 400°F (200°C).
2. Mix flour, sugar, baking powder, and salt. Cut in butter until crumbly.
3. Add cream, egg, and vanilla. Mix until dough forms.
4. Shape into a disk, cut into wedges, and bake for 15–18 minutes.

Churros with Chocolate Sauce

Ingredients:

For the churros:

- 1 cup water
- 2 tbsp sugar
- ½ tsp salt
- 2 tbsp butter
- 1 cup flour
- 1 egg
- Oil for frying

For the coating:

- ½ cup sugar
- 1 tsp cinnamon

For the chocolate sauce:

- ½ cup heavy cream
- 4 oz dark chocolate

Instructions:

1. Heat water, sugar, salt, and butter until boiling.
2. Stir in flour and cook until dough forms a ball.
3. Remove from heat, add egg, and mix well.
4. Pipe into hot oil and fry until golden.
5. Toss in cinnamon sugar.
6. Heat heavy cream and pour over chopped chocolate, stirring until smooth.

Madeleine Cakes

Ingredients:

- ½ cup butter, melted
- ¾ cup sugar
- 3 eggs
- 1 cup flour
- 1 tsp baking powder
- 1 tsp vanilla
- Zest of 1 lemon

Instructions:

1. Beat eggs and sugar until fluffy.
2. Fold in flour, baking powder, vanilla, and zest.
3. Stir in melted butter.
4. Fill madeleine molds and bake at 375°F (190°C) for 10–12 minutes.

www.ingramcontent.com/pod-product-compliance
Lightning Source LLC
LaVergne TN
LVHW081504060526
838201LV00056BA/2933